Deaf Heaven

OTHER BOOKS BY
GARRY GOTTFRIEDSON

100 Years of Contact (1990)

In Honour of our Grandmothers (1994)

Glass Tepee (2002)

Painted Pony (2005)

Whiskey Bullets (2006)

Skin Like Mine (2010)

Jimmy Tames Horses (2012)

Chaos Inside Thunderstorms (2014)

deaf heaven

POEMS

Garry Gottfriedson

RONSDALE

RONSDALE PRESS
3350 West 21st Avenue
Vancouver, B.C., Canada V6S 1G7
www.ronsdalepress.com

Typesetting: Julie Cochrane, in New Baskerville 11 pt on 13.5
Cover Design: Julie Cochrane
Paper: Enviro 100 Edition, 55 lb. Antique Cream (FSC) — 100%
    post-consumer waste, totally chlorine-free and acid-free

Ronsdale Press wishes to thank the following for their support of its publishing program: the Canada Council for the Arts, the Government of Canada through the Canada Book Fund, the British Columbia Arts Council, and the Province of British Columbia through the Book Publishing Tax Credit Program.

Library and Archives Canada Cataloguing in Publication

Gottfriedson, Garry, 1954–, author
    Deaf heaven / Garry Gottfriedson.

Poems.
Issued in print and electronic formats.
ISBN 978-1-55380-449-9 (print)
ISBN 978-1-55380-450-5 (ebook) / ISBN 978-1-55380-451-2 (pdf)

    I. Title.

PS8563.O8388D43 2016   C811'.6   C2015-906706-5   C2015-906723-5

At Ronsdale Press we are committed to protecting the environment. To this end we are working with Canopy (formerly Markets Initiative) and printers to phase out our use of paper produced from ancient forests. This book is one step towards that goal.

Printed in Canada by Marquis Book Printing, Quebec, Canada

to my niece
Andrea Aleck
& my sister
Joanne Gottfriedson

"Because who would believe the fantastic and terrible story of all of our survival, those who were never meant to survive."

— JOY HARJO

CONTENTS

– Two-Faces –

– Stigmata –

– Whisper Talk –

– Possibilities –

- Two-Faces -

Moral Standards

draw in the chorus of howls
long fought for release
hiding beneath black robes
and in solemn sermons
caching documents
in god's confession boxes

when the consecrated men were exposed
moral bankruptcy was no longer
in question — delusional
claims of justification
and faith tucked in the dark wedges
between sweaty legs
imagining the neat corners of beds
in school dorms
making the sign of the cross
completing the trip to dorms
because god equipped them
with superior moral standards
that allowed them
to be free of sin

and those who cruise
skid row in Mercedes
don't know why
the destitute child seeks
salvation in the piss-riven streets
a needle dangling from their palm
a fist coiled in sloppy war
crossed-over feet spiked
down with decades of holy sins
while the selection of popes
follows Darwin's theory of evolution

nor do the salvation seekers
know those queens and survivors
carry the weight of the Vatican
in their wombs and rectums
even believing
rape was legitimized by god

it is hard to imagine, even accept
that the purple cocks of priests
were the toys they played with
their Jesus-like entrapment
nailed to their skins
and they smell, not of droplets of blood
dripping from the heart
but the stink of their predators' sperm
crusted in private places

Indian country is full of witnesses
while the city folk spout racist rhetoric
smothering the healing songs
and losing the hope
they can't even imagine

Digestion

sometimes enemies
eat their own fanciful words
to keep wars alive

Vancouver Snapshots

Vancouver parks
busy with pimps pushing
raw deals and bows
ready to sling a needle-full of pleasure
that take down hunter and game clomping
420 speed along piss trails
fronting east-side soup lines
on a bellyful of Chinatown cures

time is meaningless
the day is meaningless
crack-house refugees
sleep away the fix
dream of drag-queen runways
handyman shooting
galleries and decaying
Pickton slaughter houses

the line space between East Hastings
and Robson Street dazzles the glamour kings
riding high on Banana Republic taste buds
but it will never be home
to sidewalk Indians, twisted cowboys and broken women
fixated on billboard pictures and Gucci pretty boys
window shopping as a cruel sidewalk dance
as the beat goes on and on

it is easy to lose one's stride here
just as it is easy to offend high fashion
terrorize it, in fact, with scar-stitched eyes
and knives protruding from hearts barely beating
all it takes is a walk to the other side
betrayal lives on the line
between skid-row
and consumer enchantment

where sushi maidens stare saucer-eyed
at Indians who escaped museums
where cowboys were hung up
on bulls too hard to ride
and where broken women crumbled in their skins
people turn away
ignore that things are real
for fear is a mania of its own

yet there's got to be hope
somewhere in the windy sky
tunnelled between the skyscraper glass
with love-palaces jetting into the sky
blocking heaven's view
canyons of isolation
stifling a society surviving
on feather-light optimism

Vancouver's new-ageism and dirty secrets
are targets for writers like me
the Pacific's knife edge
offers both the exquisite and the hideous
it brims with covert snapshots
in photo albums tucked amid Stanley Park totem poles
the relocated bones of Indigenous populations
and the Chinatown sojourners

the decades of reconstruction
the digging and re-building
hide only the prominent
meant to bury the ugly
and rebuild an attractive mosaic
worthy to sell to the world
and it does
at world-class rates

the influx of Asians is no longer
the slaves who worked the railway
when the colonies dropped
New Westminster as its rose
now they are the ones
who enslave
the Canadian psyche
demanding their place in Canada

the wealth, the symbol, the prestige of freedom
gladiator football stadiums
shining blades of hockey enforcers
Canada Place — the polished jade, the pride of Vancouver
thumps in the hearts of jaw-locking believers
driving them to drunkenness
to madness
driving them driving them

this city full of snapshots . . . snap shots

Guns and Words

these shadow words
blackness between the spaces of teeth
bold and raw barnacles sticking to gums
that make the Canadian stutter
since truth is hidden behind lips
and across this mosaic land
a crop of lies — Canada's
bequest to the world

and I have given my life
I am the mixed blood of contempt
the reminder of the white man's survival in the fur trade
the curse of my original ancestors
yet my mother's people put me on a mountain
so that my own salvation would drip
from the sweat and tears I offered as prayer
to build a future for my Secwepemc grandchildren

no vision was offered
but the words of my ancestors
streamed from my mouth
using the weapon of the white man
to speak the sounds of my blood
into an English-speaking world
because what is believed
is the ink that splatters on paper

even though I am nothing
and have nothing
only volcanic poetry
will you still point a gun at me?

Fear Traps

i

across this land the wanderer
stops or begins at the coast
piecing together a computer-based image
of Manhattan — the city of Picasso buildings
skyscraper mountains raining
yellow piss on Wall Street
on the streets leading to the ocean
where in time past, troops of Native warriors opened
their loving arms, their loving legs to immigrants
where the golden sky of morning
pours hope on the bald heads of white men
who sought western love but found slavery instead

the booby traps of political policy
founded nations for the KKK in the south
and here in the north, white supremacy runs wild
from rattlesnake mouths hissing
at women and Indigenous folk who laboured to
protect those starving and disease-stricken men
when they arrived to give birth
to another imposter European nation
so easily they forgot about their hunger
led astray from the true
meaning of the Two-Row Wampum
stitching a border for Canada and the US

ii

now here in Vancouver —
a jewel for the immigrant eye
the sun goes down on the Pacific
fog paints the city silky grey
shadows of madmen dart in and out
of streets bogged down with
the needles of the homeless
screaming racist vulgarity
because of the displacement of Native warriors
because of the Asian influx
because of the foreign policy
because multiculturalism is rhetoric

this land, this holy land
has implanted cataracts in blameless visitors
given them permission to be bigoted
because no one is good enough
nothing is good enough
except computers
the digital chips forcing
worldwide websites to sizzle
in a brogue of love letters to fill files
of computer-based love alerts
from east to west, and west to east
in a never-ending heartbreak

iii

the fear traps of an ever-distant utopia
at the forefront of every lonely person's thought
of lunatics clinging to fraught hope
as they reach for their lifelines
punching digits in desperation
just in case a warm body is willing to travel
over mountains and prairies and badlands
over swamps and rivers and lakes
doing anything it takes to reach heaven
and when heaven cannot be reached
there is always another warm body
to search for on the rain-slicked streets

or else along gravel roads
leading to mountains of desolation
in the winter's hard grasp
where the wanderer's dream dies hard
where reality is the razor blade
splitting the spirit in two
it is neither spiritual nor significant
it is the mundane business of life
it is the scent of summer death
it is the colour of red leaves in fall
waiting for the white of winter
to end it all

Hard Times

day after day he struggles in old age
along the rez roads pushing his walker
step by step with his one good leg

he has learned to move slowly
to mind his own business
rehearsing the old stories

for years he has endured and ignored
insults from the rez boys
who don't know his life

before they were born
his mother gave birth to him
in a ditch he passes daily

no one asked
about the time he got drunk
and rolled into a fire at Kirby's Point

he burned his own
leg to amputation
hardening his soul

the scars on his sunken face
a hard-times map
for these boys

who can't follow
but sometimes try
to find an elusive freedom

CFOs

man or woman
only money numbers
that can't paint pictures
of children in schools
or see the tatters of elders
in bare existence
when the CFO is the artist

this means
the rez will remain
in status quo
like a mid-evil dream
and those who create
the Excel sheets
too tongue-tied
to see beyond their dollar terms

CFO: Chief financial officer

Pretty Words

in a world gone wrong
suffocating egos sacrifice
the lives of children

it is not about purpose anymore
it is about the sperm
that spawns corporations

money mutters and consoles
when a vasectomy is done
for the sake of a childless world

the chatter dies leaving
future generations
a still-born epilogue

pretty words are for politicians
wine-drunk on egos forgetting
children make all things right

Reality

"I wanna go home," sings Michael Bublé
playing over the radio
at the JJ Bean café on Robson Street

the city's pulse is a home
full of miscalculations
thinking only of the self
but beyond cities
the unimaginable exists

yet the men sip coffee
drone out songs of hope
giggle over sloppy Canadian conversation
the space between their world
and the other, an immensity

home is the abduction of young women in Chad
waged in the weight of useless wars
this does not enter the conversation
in a room full of glass windows
where Braque-like images distort reality

Canadian cafés are full
of empty people and hungry sounds
bacon and eggs sizzling
on grills behind walls
where headaches are born

this poem was born there, too,
watching men march off to work
leaving behind condemned words

Deaf Heaven

silver words fill
the ears of downcast angels
roaming a deaf heaven

so soft is the prayer
like a winter snow
silent and powerful

on earth, heartaches are meant
to die screaming
the sounds meant to reach angels

be that as it may,
deep within the soul
hope flickers

Guilty

chaos by obscene chaos
another desire is birthed
so aflame is the tyrant's craving
to singe the words of our women
the last breath let loose
cupped in killing hands
along isolated highways
a mind full of sweaty anticipation
a body alive swirling

tear by red tear
another heart breaks
a nation of women tugging at grief
tribes of men coil anger in raw fists
children leave
the lights on at night
crawl into the hard
corners of soft minds
clinging to sanity in an insane world

brick by black brick
another wall rises
wedging revulsion between tribes and government
condoning criminal behaviour
expanding white history
denying this travesty as truth
building a sociopathic fortress
and behind it all —
a guilty prime minister

Fools

the dispossessed soul's sordid tale reeks
aching with decades of repression
a disorder of affection with amazing perfume
perhaps hiding a feminist front or macho spine

it's time to face love gone wrong
dismantle the sophisticated vogue
that created the hierarchy of denial
driving a fool's hunger

cities overflow with the frenzied already
cars honk all night long on drag streets
drunks' fists fly into the made-up faces
anger is a flag of jealous victory waving high

but the duped search for heaven's face
reach out to angels, begging forgiveness
meaning it at least for the moment
so forget about crying on Sunday mornings

religion is a big business
not about saving souls
but about building golden tombstones
on which perpetuity is engraved in marble hearts

writing such words is a risky business
for challenging beliefs is dangerous
since poets are misconstrued magicians
juggling love and hate and blather

Band Elections

our band elections
with their not-so-funny words
we'll never know hope

Pretender

his dirty smile
impels, bends and churns
belly talk

he thinks he has a gut full
of warrior courage
but it is only a mouth
packed with political lies
a toilet bowl
needing a plunger

he claims to be "chief"
pretends he's one
shiny face, black braid and a white girl —
all to impress city folk
who are amused
by the reincarnation

born of a lie he knows
not what he knows

November

I heard angst
and offered words of prayer . . .

the trembling voice of a child begging
a deaf heaven for salvation

there is no defence
there is no fighting back

autumn nights are cold
yellow moonbeams

forcing light
through the sun-faded curtains

I heard angst
and offered words of prayer . . .

beyond my plea, beyond their laughter
from the edge of the porch light

amid the dry twigs of chokecherry trees
crisp leaves crumbled

beneath the weight
of red-neck boots

leaving the victims
for infinite anarchy

I heard angst
and offered words of prayer . . .

as round-cheeked boys belligerently
trudged to their dinner tables

to feast on turkey, cranberries and grapefruit
their plump bellies full of pride

and the child smells the aftermath
cigarette smoke and filth

in late October
November one day away . . .

Behind Barbwire

cornered Indians
moo throaty sounds
behind barbwire

bug-eyed braves
set their sights
on the open gate
fall is in the air
the butcher sharpens his knife

Forced Insight

the thing about fear
is that it can be killed twice

yanked at night
from the inside out
and so awakened
to become afraid
of dying a second

slow death
in broad daylight

Wishing Bone

there's a snake in the garden
blood on the trail
the sun seems closer
the moon too far gone

there's a voice in the sky
blackness on the horizon
bleak words rumble
lightning fills the snake's eye

there's silence in the cosmos
rocks on the ground
their bellies bleeding
the wishing bone came true

Without Him

frozen in depression
he dove to heaven via cement
blood never spilled thicker
before that day on East Hastings
seven stories high
seven stories told
but not one made sense

hearing the thud in a church
where truth is whipped into prayer
angels swung the doors open
walked through the blood below
knee-deep in bone-mangled sinew
cigarette butts, reporters and junkies
to find his garbled soul

but the one who remembered
him in love and manhood
she shuffled towards the Sunrise a few blocks away
and slumped on a worn barstool
drank into twilight
thinking of the sun-sealed life
they shared . . .

although he knew
life for an Indian woman
was never simple
and he had only street love to offer
his avowal was to roam heaven
wait for the night to return
to kiss colour back into her dreams

Norms

the world is heavy
with skulls brimming
noisy impatience

airplanes jet city to city
delivering
culture thieves

global travellers
crave soul food
for misplaced identities

tribes of families are dispossessed flowers
frantically searching, re-creating and plowing
new ground for fluttering seeds

many settle in unceded territories
where Indigenous folk have rooted
tribes of their own a thousand years before Fox was born

sorrowing brown faces and burdened hands
are weighed down with tobacco offerings
heavy with the sorrow of refusal and obligation

but the homeless cannot be blamed
for searching for something better
than the love of land they never had

- Stigmata -

Identity

I am an old squaw
fighting for my lost manhood
with your stolen words

The Sins of Other Men

men who are filled with present fears
when sexual security is the unknown
paint the world in shades of beer
and die alone with the sins of other men

men who are afraid of themselves
are willing to bludgeon the hearts
of mothers, lovers, life-givers
pushing women to the edge

men who are terrified
of the internal possibilities,
fatal attractions and secret gay desires
engage in the greatest sins of all

men who act upon their fears
fill their mouths with debauchery
and split their own purple tongues
casting aside their language

men who expel their terrors with sexual paradox
exhaust themselves in a soup of self-hate
in the guilt of the aftermath
and the lack of acceptance of themselves and others

men who are petrified of the dualities within
blame those realities on religion, lifestyle and choice
because belief has created a lie for everything
and truth is a shocking discovery to be feared

men who know themselves
understand that peace thrives
within their own God-given manhood
and it is not something beyond their own skins

Micromanagers

chief and councils are expert
micromanagers
although most have no
formal education

their expertise derives
from DC Scott
the architect of devastation
since 1879

no modern Indian would think
they diligently carry
out the work of Scott
to the core of near extinction

but they do so
with vigour and enthusiasm
perpetuating disempowerment
straight to the marrow

bureaucratic Indians have learned
jargons full of specious words
cramming them down the throats
of saucer-eyed followers

is this the hope and legacy
they wish to leave
tellqelmuc
in a world so full of promise?

---

tellqelmuc: those yet to be born

Never Spoken

when beer softens his heart
there is a long slide to climb

with his back slumped to the wall
hope seems too far gone

worshipping god
seems so wrong at this point

he thinks one more than you is too many
he thinks without colour

this is the drama of the human body
words that are unspoken

Scars

grasping
at scar tissue
mapped on bodies
is hope

the journey is not
without myth
or legend
or truth

just look
closely
at the ridges etched
in battle wounds

each one a tale
promising a future
offered to grandchildren
when the lights go out

Motorcycle Riding

I learned to ride a motorcycle
after my eighth grandchild was born

the grey in one's hair
doesn't always mean wisdom

but conquering fear is freedom
a crowning moment

the heart chicken-dances
to the vibration of wind

pushing courage to the limit
what was I thinking?

yes, I have endured the unthinkable
am alive in conquest

Crossovers

there is nothing sexy
when a man's heart
falls into a glass of beer
crying his heart out
on a day when the stars fade away

destiny is karma — it is here and now
so too quick decisions
cause the toothbrush to disappear
he's gone — she's gone
a lifeless home on a dead moon night

freedom is hope, and interest free
but the luxury for this crossover is cruel
leading to whiskey bottles and fingerprints
left on coffee tables and mirrors
and no one around for the clean up

harsh mixtures and blunt reminders
for a bad-hair morning
and a mouth full of stale words and drink
sloshing in an empty belly
is not a sexy sight after all

the signs were clear
the decisions were made
everything dissolves like ice
a heartless man, a scorned woman
the crossover is complete

Cesare Borgia

in lust he was born
with a Borgia tongue
that he blistered
driven by decadence
he was
dangerously
dexterous
believing it all
claiming it all
taking it all

in a bed full
of extravagant love-play
and waiting lies,
his cock was relentless
jetting purple power
seeking a warm home
everyone was fair game
some craved it
some loathed it
but all admired it

with his father a cardinal, then pope
he knew his essence was clout and play
growing a catholic appetite
for quest and conquest
fully aware that redemption was a given
because of his papal father
and so he led with a hard heart, his tongue
belting out a wet bundle
that grew into
absolution, blackmail

child, priest, cardinal, warrior
Cesare demanded
the Borgia clan spin
rosaries full of prayer
cupped in fists fighting
imprisonment
before God and Christ
who dripped
blood once more
for the sake of the pope

and like Christ, Cesare survives
centuries of Vatican folk stories
conquering the world
building layers
of rusty memory
cocky erotica
and holding holy
dominance
over every submissive lover
to this very day

Lucrezia Borgia

daughter of a cardinal and ever so divine
she modelled for St. Catherine
transforming the Italian Renaissance
on beds built for political power

her innocence forced into marriage
at age eleven
her father and older brother Cesare
killing the unlucky husband

consummation for loyalty
seemingly a family tradition
for power-hungry control
the husbands came and went

and at the Banquet of Chestnuts
with fifty naked courtesans
for the pleasure of Alexander VI
virility was seen to triumph

she escaped through the arts,
yet crime, debauchery and corruption
transformed her world
even in Ferrara, where she was loved

a political pawn, beautiful yet sad
who died before the age of forty
she reaches down through history
touching us all

Poetry

this world is full of dizzy thoughts
plunging from the mind
spinning hand-carved words
giving birth to insistent stanzas
but poetry is not always what it seems

in a not-so-mundane world
to write about the self is mundane
to examine the ugly is fearful
to seek the genteel is safe
it seems natural to avoid the divergent

it is easy to write of red roses in love
webs of clichés that blind the immoral
much tougher to peel away the layers
protecting the cocooned souls
hiding in silken webs

no, poetry is not for the dull
nor should be written so
there is meaning in seeing what can be seen
the veil must be lifted
when ink etches paper

Heaven

she hides behind
baggy clothes
by shameful power
deeply obscured

they all gossip
in back rooms
behind her back
at the coffee table

in this space and time
she thinks
of gentle words
to fill their mouths

but there is little
she can do
to silence
obsessive tongues

so she contemplates
roaming round
heaven all day
sporting a cloak of beauty

Landed

a fly buzzed around
landed on my tear-stained face
more old senseless words

Boundary Lines

climbing through the barbwire
fence on a rez boundary line
is a back-stabbing experience
when the intention is to check
heifers on the other side

cussing crazy words
and trying to make
money grow
from beneath the hides of cows
is a skin-piercing delivery

but for a rez cowboy
an outta-bounds heifer
is an intriguing piece of meat
to sink one's teeth into
despite the risks

His Time Ran Out

for Brody

no one thought
his last ride
on the C-train
would lead him
to a fiery death
on the cold streets
of Calgary

there will be
another half-assed
investigation
dropping fancy phrases
in media flashes
and then like his death
it will all die down

but here on the rez
he will not be forgotten
'cause across this land
there are reminders of him
in the memories of those he left behind
and though his time ran out
his shadow looms

Casts

hard-luck stories delight the deprived

masks insulate the torment
at the expense of others
so odd is human nature

it wasn't always that way

dangerously glossy words are a rush
sliding past whitened teeth at the dinner table
dismissing the concern of others is fair game

the rules continually change

stone-faced talkers muddle the mundane
bringing on the smirks
adoring the destruction

instability cracks the code . . .

in a war of words, don't speak of personal matters
heartaches heal slower than broken bones
silence is a better choice

let what is to be, be . . .

- Whisper Talk -

Star Quilts

when the weak light of morning appears
the stars are not what they were

they are memory a million years old
woven into Star Quilts

each thread is a declaration
from someone in our past

our stories and lives are stitches of celebration
interlaced in a span of lifetimes

they are the colour of love and war
and the natural hue of our skins

the smell of grandmothers and grandfathers
breathing those stories into our blood

the taste of our mothers' milk
the callused hands of our fathers silken on our cheeks

it is our purpose for being parents
for the living warmth of our children just born

and so when daylight is finally here
we wrap our newborn in freshly made Star Quilts

and remember

The House

the house that protects the dreamer
is a mansion where walls speak in whispers
floors creak and bend with prayer and hope
the ceiling echoes reassurance
the tables are heavy with bannock and raspberry jam
the tea kettle whistles granny's song

the house that protects the dreamer
is a pit-house where the center fire crackles a legacy
spoken to grandchildren sitting cross-legged
on the land, where grandpa's people roamed
where for generations the smoke bears witnessed to history
the timber and bones building the dreamer's foundation

the house that protects the dreamer
is a forest full, a silent healer
where generations of healers prayed for
rebirth beneath the canvas of birch and pine
speaking to the Sky World
for the return of our land's soul

Cselmintwecw

the story of horses
is the story of my people

the tales of horses
etched in the hoof-beaten trails

the imprints speak of loud history
passed through song and dance

stsinem ell melcem
holding the branding irons

my people stamped their presence
on the skin of this land on horseback

our horses offered ceremony
and pure strength to remind us

that the blue copper of blood is resilient
souls galloping in our veins, like theirs

when we talk of them,
we talk of ourselves

clinging to the dust of our ancestors for eternity
reliving *ck'ul'tn* from season to season

so when the yellow leaves fall,
our thickening coats will protect our blood lines

and when the land sleeps white
the cold will remain on the outside

and when the land awakens to green once again
when our Mother is full with offerings
we know this is the time for *cselmintwecw* —
riding double, compassion

---

cselmintwecw: riding double on horseback
stsinem ell melcem: songs and dances
ck'ul'tn: our way of life

Mother Bears

my mother was Bear
slapping
the ground in front of me
blocking the path
I was about to go down
she stood
solid
before me in a world where
earthquakes are born

instead, I counted stars
on cloudy nights
sniffing out a trail that led
to bright lights
picking up
the scent of beer and sex
willing to cut the roots
she planted
to ground her family

I made my escape
as she lay sleeping
for the skies cleared
a full moon appeared
and lit a path
silvered with sweet promise
and I followed
the river down to the sea
an underground city of pain

and in a ditch den
I dug for myself
in a back-room bar
I heard soothing words
a hungry mother's hunting song
deeply longing and
echoing far
through the city's streets
back to the rez

so I followed
the familiar sound
of my mother
home

Stomas

we are all sons and daughters of natural disaster
there will be no moon tonight to glitter on our skins
and the winds have calmed our soulful words
reality is ugly, but survival is brilliant

as brothers and sisters, we tasted the salt
that sprang from the womb and from our eyes
as sons and daughters, we searched for relatives
from ocean's edge to edge

the salt waters are insistent and endless
discoveries of failed carcasses
washing up against our callused feet
those that did not make it to the seas' depths

the violence in the atmosphere is toxic
our blood is copper, our skin rawhide
a lethal brew of toxicity and climate change
but our vision is sharp, even in darkness

the fossils of our organs will someday be studied
the findings elaborated on the line of evolution
the morphology of survival is smuggled through time
which has forgotten the humble survivors

our secrets hide in the stomas of the world
strategizing for a new world to come
our hidden relatives are capable of colonizing
in the same pale shadows of the self

Sky Woman

the woman who fell
from the sky
spiralled to earth

with a thunderous
outcry of heart melodies
splashing in the salt sea

across the horizon
she cracked
open the clouds to rain

pouring out
songs of hope
for those yet to be born

Cabin Fever

when the January winds force
our being into madness,
the mind is full of leaves budding in spring
somewhere over the drifting snow
southern warmth is promised

words of solace frozen on tongues
seal in quivering aches
the snow sparkles
so loud is the depth of winter
ears crave silence

the soul is locked in with cabin fever
rest will not cure the fatigued spirit
but chicken soup and bannock sit waiting
the earth will soon melt into shades of green
a time for growth — a time to release madness

Atonement

she hung her head
gravity pulling
at her greying hair
as she dropped tears
on the church floor

nothing is laid to rest
on the lord's day

people with hard faces sang
out of tune
to the soaring words
of "Amazing Grace"
kleenex passed from hand to hand

and for a brief moment
she believed in atonement

These

are ear-catching words
giving meaning to tongue
sending something strong and powerful
for those yet to be born

these pretty things
these pretty words
these pretty stories
these pretty songs

are caged between the palate
and the jaw perched
like early morning birds
chattering to the young ones

these pretty things
these pretty words
these pretty stories
these pretty songs

are woven in our skins
fleshing our skeletons
speaking through our hands
born of old sounds

these pretty things
these pretty words
these pretty stories
these pretty songs

are wrapped around
saskatoons and wind-dried salmon
feeding generation to generation
reaching the ears of those yet to be born

Always Remembering

for Loretta S.

the young leave too young
it is not supposed to be this way

their whispered secrets
are the last they breathe

reminders of the rugged roads travelled
the heartbreak of mothers

so crazy is the unknown
the unexpected

the things that eat our blood
the cancers that eat our bones

no one expects
their child to die before them

but do we remember?
yes, we remember it all

Sunrise to Sunrise

sunrise to sunrise
limbs and blades stretch
to an awakening across this land

new insights fill the eyes
sparkle through a generation
that sees things as they are

poems and paintings alert
the public to what is
the response — always a surprise

language is born from the land
sung into the ears of clan members
for the beginning was original thought

this is why
when the land begins to show itself
at first light, we know who we are

Kemtsene'tkwe

when I tasted your sweetness
for the first time

at *te' kemtsene'tkwe*
I savoured your soft rumbles

your humming over rocks
over the land where my ancestors also drank

this is where my journey began
where I found devotion

my soul was melting ice
awakening near *sete'tkwe*

you are my blood
my beloved body

how can I ever leave you?

---

te' kemtsene'tkwe: the head waters
sete'tkwe: the river

Singing Songs

murmuring waters trickle
towards the lake
near my mountain home

bleeding into creeks, then rivers
where whispers die
and screams are born

onward to oceans
marking salmon maps
so they can return home

my grandmothers sat
at those waters
singing words of praise

Secwepemc Salmon Songs
that I sing today
to my grandchildren

each time they hear
breathing from this land
my grandchildren know

our voices come from
the waters of our mothers
strong breath words

offering Secwepemc singing songs
remembering the waters
of our birth

Secwepemcu'llucw

she carries his bones
along the vein of trails
where his grandmothers'
moccasin-covered feet
wore away the earth
generations before him
a labour of love

she carries his bones
kicking up the dust
singing the old songs
and remembering
lingering sage and balsam
Secwepemcu'llucw
where the land was built of bones

Secwepemcu'llucw. Land of the Secwepemc (Shuswap)

The Beginning

my life began
in the sacredness of a woman

I was protected
and grew

from within
the blood and water of my mother

the croon of ancient songs
entered her womb

I ate
what she ate

I travelled
where she travelled

I remained
within her

until my spirit
wanted to touch sky

only she remembers
the pain

Crazy Space

from the middle of nowhere
my father's counsel resonates
with profound impact

his voice is alive
and I want to hear
his stories relived

but between shifting thoughts
my mother sings ancient songs
she never allowed me to forget

my brothers are also there
and I remember their words
building courage though I am weak

this crazy space is on either side
I wonder if they remember
anything that I have said

Serenity

our potential
reaches fulfillment
when leaves fall dying

natural evolution
before snowflakes
cover yesterday

the sound of sunflowers
bending lucent words
as they drop petals

the silence of prayer
when it is wept
in a smudge bowl of fog

the hope
that the coldest day in winter
brings the promise of serenity

Born

he thinks
about the woman who gave
life to him

her waiting womb
full of water
ready to burst

life
broken
at first breath

the first words spoken
were never heard
when he was born

Courage

for Andrea Aleck

she inhales deeply
gasping at fears
taking the first step
into an unknown journey

her tired eyes focus
beyond the darkness of cancer
squeezing prayer
from her suffocating chest

offering words of praise
filled with hope in the dim light —
an old soul stepping forward
as so many do

Winds

and so when trees bow
to the weight of wind
the reply is implicit

here comes rain
here comes snow

and so a forest of whispered sounds
weave the calling
from branch to branch

here comes rain
here comes snow

and so slick is the coming
the skies noiselessly bleed fuchsia
but then the whisper winds shout grey

here comes rain
here comes snow

and so the long sleep of winter
awakens naked limbs in spring
and life pulses in the fullness of being

– Possibilities –

Lost Dog Road

I thought I had released you
from memory, but at this moment

the bees buzzing in my stomach
shoot their arrows

I smell you on my skin, remember the taste of you
that July day when the sun was stuck in the sky

tonight the south wind carries your scent
as I lay to rest your image on pillows soft as down

and I am certain you have seen yourself in books of poetry
I have written and sold at Indian markets when times were good

if you did see them, I will tell you
they were written the time I travelled on Lost Dog Road

the poems fell out of my mouth, tooth by tooth
and they were my release long before I was born again

Birds Tangled in Wire

from across the room
from across the landscape
from across his throat vowels

Cohen's simple words
unravel his gnarled songs
like birds tangled in wire

a bird himself, fluttering in shadows
sneak-peeking at cracked mirrors
he writes of abandoned rooms

he sees the pieces of himself
scribbled on the dry landscape of paper
with pens running dry

lying on dust-filled floors
he also chokes to find his voice
to write as Cohen did

from across the room
from across the landscape
from across his throat vowels

he sings once more . . .

3 A.M.

it is 3 in the morning
my mind is full of your poetry
song lines that don't sleep
you are probably dreaming
astounding silence

but throughout my home
the furnace rumbles
disrupting metaphors
interfering with imagery
my bones ache

daylight comes slowly in late September
but swift possibilities in dawn's oyster sky
answer to this awakening
as poetry to be written
in the full light of day

I sip a cold cup of coffee
an abundance of black sweetness
page after page
image after image
poetry to be read in springtime.

Scalping Mad

scalping mad
the knife wedged
between pearly teeth
and ugly words sharp
enough to pierce
beyond goodness

but in a future time they are also
a flutter of winter birds
returning home

listen closely
do you hear them?
they are slow love songs
humming in the wings of wind
strong enough to make
even the sharpest knife dull

Time Alive

the stomach of clocks
tick away

seconds turn to decades
time has no pity

it takes a significant event
to keep memory alive

milestones etching
wrinkles in the skin

echoes of footsteps
walking across floors

a floral bouquet unexpectedly
hand-delivered

soul mates murmuring love phrases
at contentment's peak

the exhilaration of a first-born
coddled in the sky of open palms

the heartbreak
when a loved one is released

moments alive
that churn in the guts of time

Songs

somewhere there is a love-bird song
playing on the radio for everyone

singing words jiving body love
for people everywhere

it was all about a strand of her hair
skating across his pounding chest

even though he was not a Brad Pitt
nor she an Angelina Jolie

they knew this was their song
finite and infinite

Conversations

sometimes
I want
to eat
poetic
conversation

and chew
on the image
that brought
you here
in the first place

He Left

with every light on
crumbs of bread still
speckling the counter tops
a cup half full of milky coffee
the aroma lingering lightly amid
the broken pieces of a message written
quickly on scraps of torn envelopes smeared blue
the weapon, a pen, announcing heartache, rolled to the floor
shades of grey beams streaming between the kitchen and porch

he left
at dusk alone
with a duffle bag
the dressers half full
of his clothing, the scent of him
spread thick on the towels, his toothbrush
sticky with paste and spit, the bathroom in disarray
the bed unmade, the laundry piled, socks still on the floor
hangers tangled like the lives they led before the lights went out

Maroon Five

drowning in a puddle of my own nerves
I struggled to crawl out of my own recklessness

clinging to "Misery" and the dry edge of salvation
I listened to the falsetto and timbre of Adam Levine

hearing his singing tones in the density of muddy mayhem
I know the resurrection forever more was mine

His So-Called Love

streaming through
the nothing of his white mouth
came the specious words

"three aboriginal children
we have raised
we know the Indian heart
and how to break down barriers"

his love is a raging fever

I wonder
if he could hear me speak
a love that was birthed in my mother's womb
where I first learned to walk in water?

Indigenous nations' bellies are full of hope

but it has never been
easy to find a way
around daddy
so late at night

this is an insane war

my heart has seen
so many eyes alight
with the queen's currency
who blame those who protect themselves

insidious yammer

I am not sure
if he can swallow this poem
or spit back another

Rainstorms

I sit on a hillside
in a collage of bunchgrass and rocks
overlooking unmarked valleys below me
behind is Saddle Mountain — only a name
close to the mountain's edge
where earth meets sky
creeping grey clouds bring
news of rain

rain everywhere in my heart
left behind during storms
in the Rockies or Main Street bars
people lose themselves
in bunchgrass and rocks
between beers and lovers
on the streets in Winnipeg or Vancouver
in the Rockies or on Saddle Mountain

but rain doesn't hurt
it comes to wash away the blues
I heard harsh words before
mixed in with the crinkled sheets at dawn
after long sleepless nights
and butt-filled ashtrays
on café table tops where old men sing the blues
and meet for all-day-long coffees

but blue could really be black
coffee hitting stomach bottom
seeping its way through the body
or the colour of eyes
reflected in my mind
bringing me to this hillside
sitting in rainstorms
with hope gathering

One-Sided Love

people with sharp edges
spend too much time
on one-sided love

it's a cock blocker
a story told and retold
with far too many variables

bending the fingers backwards
breaking the backs of pens
trying to dig up seductive words

but when the music comes falling
lifting up from the other side
a new song softens the edge

Chance

for all the "nevers" said at night
the moon slips
unexpected pleasing words

in the dimness of love
the tummy is full
of seeding sunflowers

when the moon comes too close
the Wildman in him blossoms
taming words

blushing hope sparkles in his eyes
not from the moon's glow
but from the stars when they found a home in him

Koyoti Tricks

Koyoti itched
to drop his secrets in ink
lay it all out on the skins of trees
oral traditions were not good enough
but divine revelations might do the trick

language is a learned skill
thought Koyoti
to transcribe the secluded and private
but his mind drifted after the sun goes down
when the fun begins

dog-trotting Koyoti bragged
he was a pro at body love
not only with his tongue
but at the edge of his paws
where tricks aroused dancing dreams

he paw-picked lines
on the smooth bole of trees
giggling fancy words
thinking of the moon's warmth
on his soft fur

he hunkered down
in the raw heat of erotic stories
nattering to himself in the turquoise of night
into yellow dreams groping
far beyond his expectations

but in the clarity of sunlight
the landscape never lies
truth lies naked for all to see
no matter what trickster tale
Koyoti may tell

Bombs

there are bombs
in our bodies
private and calm
easily detonated
causing tender storms

it is the breath
that pushes past
everyday conversation
with precise aim
to target the soft spots

brushing soft purrs
caressing the curve of the neck
working its way to ears ablaze
like caterpillars inching their way
along the smooth stem of dandelions

each breath is a lip murmur
causing skin tremors
fueling profusion
waiting for explosions
to signal amatory flight

slurping nectar is the raw
sweetness of pleasure
the finger in motion
knowing exactly
where detonation occurs

it has always been this way
since the beginning of time
bombs
helpless
bombs . . .

Cool Cats

cool, way-too-cool cats
strut pussy-footed into the room
sleek and fine

cool, way-too cool cats
mouth-licked shiny fur
without permission

cool, way-too-cool cats
meow mouths full of purring words
almost believable

cool, way-too-cool cats
scamper away at the unexpected
bruised and crushed

cool, way-too-cool cats
fired of porcelain china
delicate and easily hurt

Body Love

fingers stroke over moist skins
like waves on a lake

skin-hungry bodies moan
to penetrating pink surrender

the sharp cry of the erotic
leading to liberation

heightened when the sun's beams
fade the moon into silence

praying this moment doesn't end
the unity of two in body love

Hands

I see the aged skin lines
making memory maps
on these hands of mine
crooked like cedar roots
spiralling like the prayers
pulled out of my maimed heart

who would think these hands
could speak words of love when needed?

many times they have ridden
over rocks and hard ground
on buggies and horses
who have galloped off to cities
leaving my thighs empty
my hands without purpose

when times were tough
my hands have done the thinking for me

they were scraped raw
exposing pure bone
but found victory from time to time
even in the wildest places
where the hair of horses quivered pleasure
when these hands rode from sky to touch warm earth

these hands have journeyed
over lives to leave this story

Bees

be a man
be a man

    stare sexy
    stare sexy

be a woman
be a woman

    beg baby
    beg baby

be a man
be a man

    rakish words
    rakish words

be a woman
be a woman

    laughing eyes
    laughing eyes

be a man
be a man

    get me hard
    get me hard

be a woman
be a woman

    tummy flowers
    tummy flowers

Romeo and Skalula

on nights when the moon comes close
it brings out Skalula
snarling lusty and seductive
dreaming up love and wars for the young

on nights like this Romeo lives in poetry
as the land spreads wild perfumes
while Skalula lurks in the skulls
of mad men and lovers

filled with longing Romeo climbs the ladder of night
to join with his beloved
hanging on the neck of those who surrender
the insane one growls victory

Skalula hides his weapons in boyhood dreams
wrapped around youthful memories
while Romeo knows the weapon
of a caress on a full-moon night

the opposition of both
marks a place where battle shares desire
a home for dreamers
a home for darkness

Skalula: a wickedly seductive figure in Secwepmc tales

Anything-Goes Love

puppy love
panting
silly words
a promise of forever love

Koyoti love
suspended
on the long
spine of winter love

rez love
dog-trotting
fire to fire
in the spring of love

multi-cultural love
zigzagging
city to city
screaming freedom love

anything-goes love
mixing and matching
diversion or reality
in an age of much-needed love

Go-Time

at the core of fatal attraction
loving words bloom

it is natural
evolution

that man becomes
what he thinks about

and what do men think about
but go-time when the attraction dissolves

Koko Taylor

the heart of Koko Taylor
rumbles in my ears
cavernous sounds
forged in my veins
iron softened to strong affection

notes burst from the deep
rasps of desolate words
I'd rather go blind
than to see you
walk away from me

and you over there, my voice tugs at you
rasping blues songs
weepy notes escaping disbelief
lingering in your fresh scent
still on my skin

I want so badly to let you go
to scrub my body with wild rose
to cleanse myself until it is over
to offer myself humbly to the world
I want so badly . . .

Impassable

we were young
when she gave birth
to a stillborn child
at full term

I was helpless then
as I am now

in the passing years
she drank herself full of whiskey bullets
a state of perpetual mourning
clinging to dead flowers

she never returned home
sober enough to put the gun down

some things are impassable
because when pain overtakes the mind
the soul escapes the body
never to find solace

Metaphors

I've been told
I write poems with images
that reveal the common experience of others

I gave you a poem once
but you killed it

Swayback

gold barbwire
fenced my finger
loving words corralled my love
but fences decay over time
and horses grow old

the swayback bones
in my hand ache
the cold never bothered me before
but now I know
what your body was saying to mine

My Soul

for Andrea and Ron

in the darkness of day
when the sky's light crumbles
take my heart and stand by me
give me your strength

as sorrow binds me
to the grave of my greatest love
breathe quiet words
for turmoil is my only light

let me lay my broken self
near you
to hear the sweet sound of summer rain
falling upon your beating heart

take my burden
as I surrender my fears to your strengths
for every desire in my body is ready
as I raise my hands in thankfulness

hold onto a handful of sky
scarce and precious, I am humbled
that you know my movements
signs of an awakening thirst

taking your soft words
I lean into your body
close to your soul —
won't you stay with me?

ABOUT THE AUTHOR

 Garry Gottfriedson, from the Secwepemc nation (Shuswap), was born, raised and lives in Kamloops, B.C. Growing up on a ranch in a ranching and rodeo family, he has been fully immersed in his people's traditions and spirituality. He comes from four generations of horse people. His passion for horses, raising and training them, still continues to this day. He holds a Master of Education from Simon Fraser University and has studied Creative Writing at the Naropa Institute in Boulder, Colorado. His published works include *100 Years of Contact* (SCES, 1990); *In Honour of Our Grandmothers* (Theytus, 1994); *Glass Tepee* (Thistledown, 2002, and nominated for First People's Publishing Award 2004); *Painted Pony* (Partners in Publishing, 2005); *Whiskey Bullets* (Ronsdale, 2006, and Anskohk Aboriginal Award finalist); *Skin Like Mine* (Ronsdale, 2010, and shortlisted for Canadian Authors Association Award for Poetry); *Jimmy Tames Horses* (Kegedonce, 2012); and *Chaos Inside Thunderstorms* (Ronsdale, 2014). His works have been anthologized both nationally and internationally. He has read from his work across Canada and in the USA, Europe and Asia.

PRAISE FOR GARRY GOTTFRIEDSON'S POETRY

– CHAOS INSIDE THUNDERSTORMS

"Fearless in the making, Garry again emerges as one of the most beautiful voices in Indigenous country."
— LEE MARACLE, author of *Ravensong*

"We are all fortunate to learn from Garry as a mature writer who has travelled an individual road measured with experience resulting in a high form of literary practice."
— JANET ROGERS, Victoria's former Poet Laureate

– SKIN LIKE MINE

"A mesmerizing cacophony of identity. . . . *Skin Like Mine* is so finely crafted that it will fascinate new and experienced readers of First Nations literature."
— *Canadian Literature*

"A beautiful and complex collection of poems."
— *CM Magazine*

– WHISKEY BULLETS

"Heartbreakingly honest, clever and tough, Garry Gottfriedson's poetry will move your heart."
— RICHARD VAN CAMP, author of *The Lesser Blessed*